Pocahontas

By Nancy Polette

Consultant
Jeanne Clidas, Ph.D.
National Reading Consultant
and
Professor of Reading, SUNY, Brockport

Children's Press ®
A Division of Scholastic Inc.
New York   Toronto   London   Auckland   Sydney
Mexico City   New Delhi   Hong Kong
Danbury, Connecticut

Designer: Herman Adler Design
Photo Researcher: Caroline Anderson
The photo on the cover shows Pocahontas around the time of her marriage
to John Rolfe.

Library of Congress Cataloging-in-Publication Data

Polette, Nancy.
  Pocahontas / by Nancy Polette.
     p. cm. — (Rookie biographies)
Includes index.
Summary: An introduction to the life of the young seventeenth-century Indian
woman who befriended Captain John Smith and the English settlers of Jamestown.
  ISBN 0-516-22859-5 (lib. bdg.)   0-516-27782-0 (pbk.)
  1. Pocahontas, d. 1617—Juvenile literature. 2. Powhatan Indians—
Biography—Juvenile literature. 3. Jamestown (Va.)—History—Juvenile literature.
[1. Pocahontas, d. 1617. 2. Powhatan Indians—Biography. 3. Indians of North
America—Virginia—Biography. 4. Women—Biography. 5. Jamestown
(Va.)—History.] I. Title. II. Series: Rookie biography.
  E99.P85 P654 2003
  975.5'01'092—dc21

                              2002015155

CHILDREN'S PRESS, AND ROOKIE BIOGRAPHIES™, and associated
logos are trademarks and or registered trademarks of Grolier Publishing
Co., Inc. SCHOLASTIC and associated logos are trademarks and or
registered trademarks of Scholastic Inc.
1 2 3 4 5 6 7 8 9 10 R 12 11 10 09 08 07 06 05 04 03

Pocahontas was a Native American princess.

4

Her father was the great Chief Powhatan.

In 1607, the English came to Powhatan's land and built houses.

The new English colony (KOL-uh-nee) was called Jamestown. A colony has many people who have left their old homes to live in a new place.

8

The people of Jamestown liked ten-year-old Pocahontas. She did cartwheels. She ran races and climbed trees. She could climb faster than any of the other children.

Pocahontas learned English words from Captain John Smith, the leader of Jamestown. Pocahontas and John Smith became good friends.

11

Pocahontas made many trips to Jamestown. She saw that the English people had trouble growing crops. They did not know how to hunt.

She asked her father to send corn and deer meat. With her help, the people of Jamestown had more food to eat.

Pocahontas did a brave thing when she was twelve years old. She saved her friend John Smith.

John Smith was caught by Native Americans and brought to Chief Powhatan. First, the chief welcomed him. He had traveled far from Jamestown to look for food.

16

Then, two Native Americans made him lie down on large stones. They raised their heavy clubs.

Pocahontas cried out!

She threw herself on John Smith.
She held his head in her arms.
The Native Americans put
down their clubs. They let John
Smith go.

Did they really want to kill John
Smith? No one knows for sure.

Years later, Powhatan told the English people that they must give him guns for food. The English would not give him guns.

Powhatan took some of the English people and would not let them leave.

Pocahontas was 18 years old now.

A captain of a ship knew that Pocahontas was a princess. He tricked her into coming on his ship. He took her to Jamestown and then to another colony.

She was set free after one year.

While living with the English people, Pocahontas met John Rolfe. He was an English colonist (KOL-uh-nist). They married in 1614 and had a son.

This was the start of peace between the English and the Native Americans. They did not fight.

Pocahontas and John went
to England. She met the king
and queen. Pocahontas was
21 years old.

The queen thanked Pocahontas
for helping the English in
Jamestown.

Pocahontas got sick in England. She died before she could return home.

We remember Pocahontas as the Native American princess. She showed people how to live together in peace.

Words You Know

Chief Powhatan

Jamestown colony

English people

John Rolfe

John Smith

Pocahontas

Index

About the Author

Nancy Polette, a reading consultant and former elementary school teacher, has written both fiction and nonfiction for children, including a novel and three picture books. She lives in O'Fallon, Missouri.

Photo Credits

Photographs © 2003: Corbis Images/Bettmann: 12, 31 top left; Hulton|Archive/Getty Images: cover, 3; North Wind Picture Archives: 4, 7, 11, 15, 16, 19, 23, 24, 25, 26, 29, 30 top right, 30 bottom, 31 bottom right, 31 top right, 31 bottom left.

Illustrations by Rodica Prato